UNOFFICIAL GUIDES JUNIOR

Starter Guide to Super Smash Bros.

by Josh Gregory

CH… PRESS

An…

Published in the United States of America by Cherry Lake Publishing
Ann Arbor, Michigan
www.cherrylakepublishing.com

Reading Adviser: Beth Walker Gambro, MS, Ed., Reading Consultant, Yorkville, IL

Photo Credits: Images by Josh Gregory

Cherry Lake Press is an imprint of Cherry Lake Publishing Group.

Library of Congress Cataloging-in-Publication Data has been filed and is available at catalog.loc.gov

Printed in the United States of America by
Corporate Graphics

Note from the Publisher: Websites change regularly, and their future contents are outside of our control. Supervise children when conducting any recommended online searches for extended learning opportunities.

Contents

Totally Unique

Sonic the Hedgehog is one of the many non-Nintendo characters in *Super Smash Bros.*

The first *Super Smash Bros.* came out in 1999. It was unlike anything Nintendo had ever made! Why? It was a **crossover** game. Players could choose from dozens of characters. And then fight them! For example, Mario and Luigi could face off against Pikachu from Pokémon. And Donkey Kong could battle Link from Zelda. It's no surprise that *Super Smash Bros.* became a smash hit!

The Goal

Super Smash Bros. is a fighting game unlike any other. It was first created for the Nintendo 64 (N64) game console.

Super Smash Bros. is also unique in another way. Most fighting games are based on one-on-one battles. The fighters try to hurt each other. Each attack makes them weaker. But in *Super Smash Bros.*, up to four people can fight. And their goal is to knock other players off the stage.

New Games

Super Smash Bros. once required two separate games. The "Ultimate" version of the game offers both in one package! It's played on the Nintendo Switch.

After the first *Super Smash Bros.* game, others followed. But the **concept** stayed the same. Yet each new game added more features. For example, there have been new characters, stages, and weapons. Some games allow for 8-player battles. In 2018, *Super Smash Bros. Ultimate* came out. It included more than 70 characters!

Meet the Creator

Super Smash Bros. was created by Masahiro Sakurai. He's a famous Japanese game **developer**.

Many Modes

It can take players a long time to learn every stage in *Super Smash Bros. Ultimate*.

You can explore different modes in *Super Smash Bros. Ultimate*. Some are better for solo players. Others are better for a group. Get started by choosing "Smash" from the main menu. Then choose the settings for the match. You can **customize** the rules. For example, how many lives will each player get? How long will the match last? You pick!

Which Stage?

Some stages are really unusual. One takes place on a moving train!

Next, choose a stage to battle on. Each one is inspired by another video game! You'll find stages filled with **obstacles**. Others have moving platforms. For the most basic stage, choose Battlefield or Final Destination. Getting used to each stage takes time. But there's a right stage for you. Try them all out!

The Random Option

If you can't decide on a stage, you can let the game choose! This is called the **Random** option.

Characters

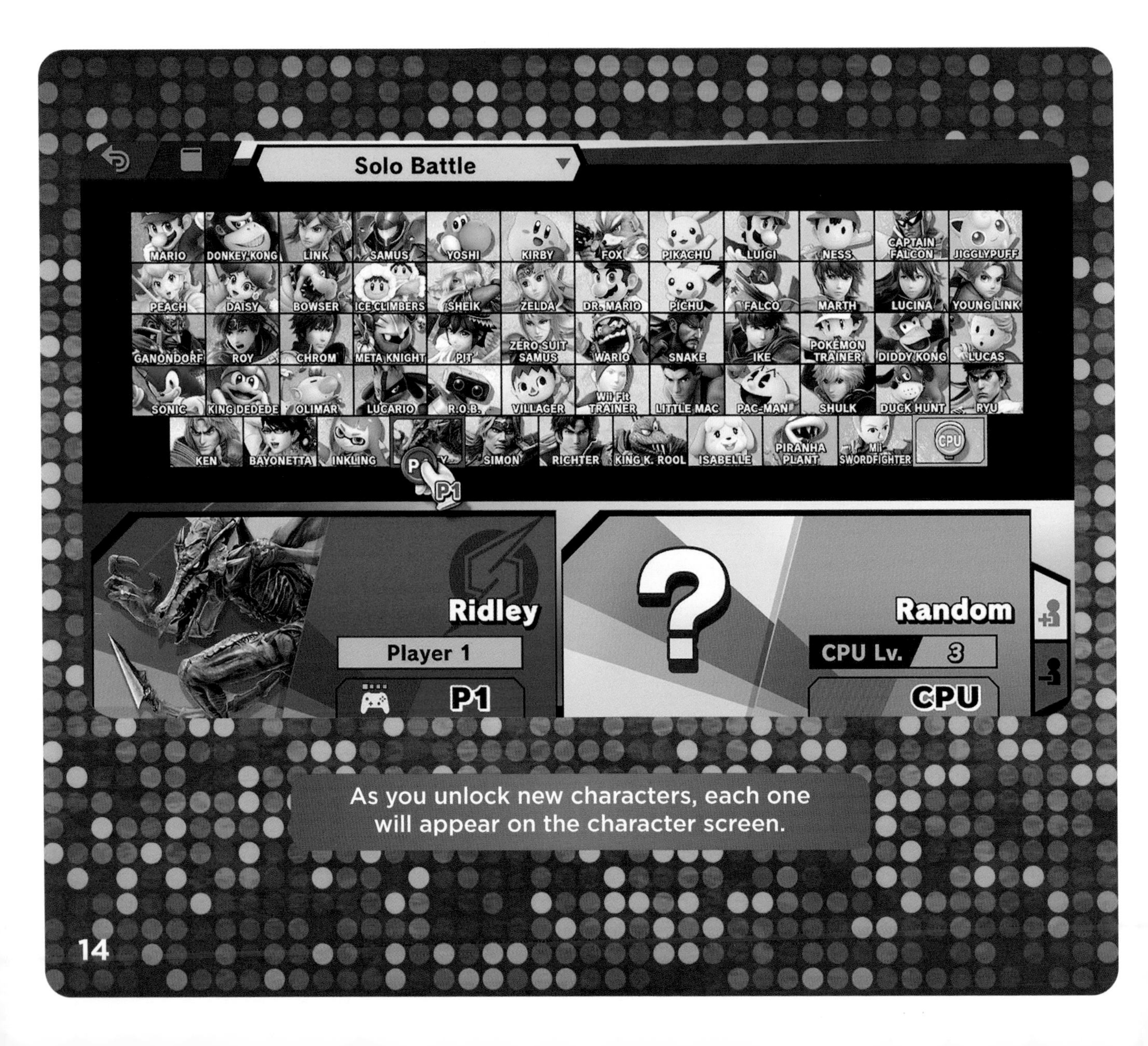

As you unlock new characters, each one will appear on the character screen.

Now, it's time to pick your character. You'll only have a few to choose from at first. As you play, many more will be unlocked. Each one has different strengths. Play well, and each can win. You can also add computer-controlled players to battle against.

Fighting Skills

You can use a shield to block damage. Do this by pressing ZR or ZL. If an enemy has their shield up, try a grab attack. It can reach right through the shield.

Once you start fighting, be smart. Damage your **opponent** as much as you can. Then knock them off the stage. Watch the bottom of the screen to see each character's damage. You can also see how many lives each player has. Use this information to help plan an attack. But be careful. Watch out for sneak attacks!

Special Moves

Hit the A button to perform regular attacks. Carry out special attacks with the B button. The exact attack depends on which direction you move the control stick as you press the button.

The Right Moves

Some items are funny—and powerful. A giant flower can be used as a dangerous weapon.

Jumping plays a very big role in *Super Smash Bros.* Press Y or X to jump. You can even jump while you're in the air! While you're bouncing, keep an eye out for items. These drop into stages at random. Some are weapons like bats or hammers. Others, like the Bunny Hood, will let you jump super high!

What's Next?

Training mode allows you to practice your skills.

Players love the intense **competition** of *Super Smash Bros.* Remember to have a good time. Winning isn't everything. You can always improve your skills in the game's Training mode. The more you practice, the better you'll be. So start playing and have fun!

Esports

Super Smash Bros. is a popular **esport**. Players compete in **tournaments**. Many thousands of fans cheer them on.

GLOSSARY

competition (kom-puh-TISH-uhn) a contest

concept (KON-sept) a general idea

crossover (KRAWS-oh-ver) being successful by reaching a bigger audience

customize (KUHS-tuh-mahyz) to build according to certain specifications

developer (dih-VEL-uh-pur) someone who makes video games or other computer programs

esport (EE-sport) a professional video game competition

obstacles (OB-stuh-kulz) things that slow down progress

opponent (uh-POH-nuhnt) a team that another team plays against

random (RAN-duhm) done without a conscious decision

tournaments (TUR-nuh-muhnts) sporting events with a series of games or rounds